WHERE THE
FISH ARE

WHERE THE FISH ARE

The New York Times
Fish-Finding Book

Leonard M. Wright, Jr.

Illustrations by Richard Ellis
and Frank Golad

Manufactured in the United States of America. Published simultaneously in Canada by Fitzhenry & Whiteside, Ltd., Toronto.

Designed by Beth Tondreau

Library of Congress Cataloging in Publication Data

Wright, Leonard M
    Where the fish are.

    1. Fishing.   I.   New York times.   II.   Title.
SH441.W74   1977   799.1   77-79048
ISBN 0-8129-0717-5

To the members of my family and my friends with whom I've fished over the years . . . some of whom I've taught, but from all of whom I've learned something about fishing.

CONTENTS

WHERE THE
FISH ARE

INTRODUCTION
Nelson Bryant

A few years ago while visiting the Triangle X ranch in Moose, Wyoming, I rode my horse to the Snake River, which was perhaps two miles away.

With the magnificent Tetons above me, I surveyed the stream from the saddle and was dismayed. It was about 60 yards across with a steep gradient and running like a mill-race. To one who had been weaned on the trout streams of New England, the Snake seemed unapproachable.

I knew that one could drift down the river in a rubber raft, taking an occasional shot at an eddy or a deep pool before being swept past, but how did one fly fish it from shore?

A companion with no more knowledge of the river than I, but with a livelier imagination suggested that I fish the undercut banks and under the fallen trees and snags along the shore. Taking the advice, I soon was fast to a 12-inch cutthroat and many more followed.

I tell of this experience because it is an example of what Len Wright's book is all about. Read it carefully and apply what you have learned and you will spend less time flailing barren water.

Volumes have been written, and will continue to emerge, on specific approaches to specific fish, and they are needed. But what Leonard Wright—an accomplished fly fisherman —has done is to offer some sound advice for almost every situation a beginning angler is likely to face, whether fresh or salt water, stream or lake.

3

One suggestion he makes that should always, if possible, be followed, is to watch or consult local anglers. When I first joined *The New York Times* as Wood, Field and Stream columnist, I was already in early middle age with a solid background in both fresh- and salt-water angling in the northeast, but, with the exception of a little trout fishing in Wales and Germany, the rest of the nation and the world was something I had only read about. With all the arrogance of what I now regard as youth, I—whether I went south to the Caribbean or north to Labrador—listened to what the anglers or the guides on the spot had to say and then did it my way.

For a few trips I was lucky, but before long I was doing very little and had to admit that the men on the scene knew more about their particular situation than I.

Timing is one of the most important factors in angling, for although you may be casting where the fish are you will do nothing if they are not feeding.

For example, if one wishes to fly fish for small—up to 12 pounds—striped bass in certain salt ponds in Massachusetts, the right time is probably in May and early June when thousands of tiny young sandworms emerge in early evening to swim about in the shallow water. And if one wishes to do the same thing with the giant tarpon of the Florida Keys one of the best times is when the palolo worms appear in profusion on or near the surface for a few days before, during and after the first full moon in June.

The time of day is often as important as the time of year. In general, fishing is best in the early morning and early evening. This often abrades the relationship between a non-angling wife and her husband, for the prime time coincides precisely with the cocktail hour and supper. The best advice one can give a young husband is to fish the early morning hours and save the remainder of the day for his family. He'll be groggy with fatigue, but will not be faced with the dreadful choice of ignoring either the rising trout or his familial pleasures and duties.

The condition of the water one intends to fish is important. If an upstream tempest has turned your favorite trout stream into a muddy torrent, stay home and mow the lawn. Or, if one is available, visit a trout pond or lake, for they—particularly if they are spring fed—do not respond rapidly to rainfall. And if a three-day onshore storm has hit your favorite surf casting beach realize that several days will pass before fish resume their normal feeding pattern. Also remember that tides are often all important when fishing salt water; and here again, one must, if not a native of the area, consult the locals.

As Mr. Wright notes, develop a keen eye for rising fish, for fish chasing bait; and on salt water, for diving terns or surface-feeding gulls. Watch for any strange disturbance on the water. I once had a splendid two hours with bluefish in the 15-pound class because I was fortunate to spot them finning—lolling about on the surface—60 yards off the beach. There were no birds about, nor were the fish chasing bait, but portions of their dark fins and tails showed above the water. Sometimes when so occupied they will not respond to anything, but on that occasion they savagely attacked the popping plugs we tossed at them.

Although Leonard Wright, as I do, obviously prefers fishing moving water for trout, angling for the species in still water—lakes and ponds—can be delightful.

In most of the northeast from spring until early June, you will have little difficulty taking trout on a fly in such waters, but when hot weather arrives the upper layer of a lake becomes super-heated, sometimes reaching 80 degrees. It is then that you must—except for the few trout that rise for flies in the shadows of the western shore near dusk—use a sinking line. And you must also locate the cold spring holes where the fish will gather. The best way I know to do this is to obtain a map of the pond and systematically drag an electronic thermometer along the bottom. When you find such a spot mark it on the map by shore ranges or by a small buoy. You can even tether the buoy just under the water if you want to keep your place a secret. Anchor 30 feet from it and fish your wet flies or nymphs through it. This applies, of course, to relatively shallow lakes or ponds that, because of the spring holes, are able to sustain a trout population.

A fly fishing friend and I once devoted most of our weekends one summer searching for such a spring hole in a mountaintop lake in New Hampshire. Most of the water in the lake—which averaged less than 10 feet deep—was above the mid-70's by late July, but in a place near the cliff-dominated north shore the water was 22 feet deep and the temperature on the bottom about 42 degrees. The brook trout must have lain in there like cordwood during the summer, for we never failed to take all the fish we wanted.

Mr. Wright has observed that after-dark fly fishing for trout sometimes produces very well (consult the laws of the state with reference to after-sundown trout fishing, by the way), and one thing to remember when fishing a stream is to get yourself into the best position for casting before darkness falls. Work the water while there is still light so you will know how much line you will need to reach the most promising spots and so you will know how much room you have got for your backcast.

When you have reached the stage that most of your peers regard you as an expert in at least one type of angling, beware of what I call the "oldtimer's syndrome": slavish devotion to one lure, fly, approach or location. The day will come when what worked last year or last month will not work today. Stay loose. Try your time-tested techniques first, but if they fail don't be averse to experimenting.

The best example that comes to mind involves the late

Al Reinfelder who, in addition to being one of the warmest men I have ever known, was a tireless, highly innovative and successful angler. There is a section of the north shore of Martha's Vineyard Island—which I have fished for over 40 years—where I cruised among the rocks close to shore in shallow water casting swimming plugs for striped bass. One year that did not work and Al suggested that we back off 300 yards from the beach where the rock-studded bottom was over 20 feet down and try the same plugs. I laughed at this, but acquiesced and within minutes we were raising and hooking big bass.

If you are a beginner, *study* Len Wright's book. It gives you the essentials of most forms of angling faster than any text I know.

If you are a veteran, read it carefully. You may be reminded of something you learned 30 years ago but forgot.

HOW TO USE
THIS BOOK

Ninety percent of your fishing problems are solved once you have discovered *where the fish are*.

Admittedly, you will not catch much when fishing the hottest trout spot in the river with a 12-inch striped bass plug. Nor can you expect to take many stripers with a gnat-sized trout dry fly. But even a beginner using any common-sense bait or lure over a concentration of fish will catch more than the expert casting over barren water.

And that is what this book is designed to do—to put you on top of the most fish, in most places, most of the time.

Suppose you are a salt-water angler who finds himself on a large, unfamiliar lake. Or suppose you are an expert stream fisherman visiting the seashore for the first time. Finding the fishy spots in the thousands of acres of water in front of you will probably seem as impossible as finding a needle in a haystack.

Not so. Almost all fish have predictable habits and habitats. Fish are utterly selfish and self-indulgent. They want either the most food, the most comfort or the most safety. Where they find all three together, they'll stack up like cordwood.

The preferred foods of the more common fresh and salt water fishes are given on pages 65 through 70 and 122 through 137. So are their comfort requirements—their tolerance to currents, temperature preferences and type of bottom or shelter they seek. The safety factor is more complicated because it varies widely from species to species and

9

from situation to situation. However, you will find many clues on places where fish feel secure scattered throughout the many "where-to" and "when-to" picture pages in the four major sections of the book.

Let us go back to that unfamiliar lake, for example. The first thing you have to find out is *what kind* of fish are in it. You may know from hearsay that it's largemouth bass and bluegill water. If not, any local resident or any hardware, tackle store or boat livery proprietor will tell you what species of fish to expect and what they usually catch them on.

If, indeed, the answer is largemouths and bluegills, turn to pages 65 and 70 for a quick look into the private lives of these two species. Now suppose again you decide to try for the larger of these two fishes, the largemouth. You now know it prefers warmish water of medium to shallow depth, likes sheltering weeds, logs or snags and has a yen for minnows, frogs and crawfish.

Your next step is to leaf through pages 35 to 53 on ponds and lakes to learn how to "read" the vast expanse of flat water in front of you. Choose the likeliest nearby place (say, that shallow cove on page 43) and begin fishing a bait or lure that closely resembles a favorite largemouth food and fish it at a depth and with the behavior typical of that type of food.

It's as simple as that.

The most successful fishermen are invariably those who can pinpoint fish-producing areas *before* they start fishing. They don't trust to trial and error. They concentrate their efforts where the fish are.

The next 150 pages are designed to give you—in a few minutes—what it could take you a lifetime to learn the hard way.

FRESH WATER

BROOKS, STREAMS, AND RIVERS

Running water differs from still water in one important way: it brings the food to the fish like an endless belt-conveyor while lake or pond fish have to cruise around and find their meals. As a result, most fish in flowing water tend to stay in or near one chosen place for days, weeks, even months because their food travels to them.

However, most fish make short trips several times a day from their secure resting places to areas where food is more plentiful. These journeys may be only several feet and are seldom more than 100 yards. Then, too, most river fish move slightly upstream as the season advances seeking temperatures more to their liking. Running water not only gets bigger as it progresses downstream; it gets warmer, too.

Most river fishes stake out a territory and defend it from all smaller or weaker rivals. Despite this, fish are constantly seeking to better their lot and steadily challenge their betters for choicer quarters. So, if you catch a good trout, for example, from a deep cut under a root tangle one evening, fish it carefully on your next outing. Another good fish is almost certain to move into this choice vacancy—often within a few hours.

Fish living in running water are usually somewhat smaller than specimens of the same species that inhabit lakes and ponds. Floods and droughts reduce their food supplies. And it takes energy that would otherwise go into growth to battle the current. But river fish undergo tougher training and usually fight harder than their still-water brethren. And, perhaps even more important, there's a special charm to flowing-water fishing that has convinced many anglers that this is the choicest fishing of all.

1. Outsides of Bends

Wherever running water changes direction, both the main thread of the current and the deeper water will be near the outside edge of the turn. This concentration of food-carrying current, plus the security of deeper water, make the outsides of bends prime fish-holding places.

2. Merging Currents

Where two currents come together, twice as much food is
carried to the fish. Wherever you find this condition, along
with reasonable depth or protective cover, you will also find
fish. In fact, fish often feed at shallow current junctions
when they feel protected by the dim light of dawn or dusk.

3. Drop-offs

Where water suddenly deepens—as at the heads of most pools—the current slows down and the food carried by the flow begins to settle to the bottom, making easy pickings for fish. Such places have everything: easy food, the safety of depth and the comfort of a moderate current.

4. Eddies

Water rushing into a pool faster than it can escape tends to form a large slow whirlpool. Fish will often position themselves where the upstream flow starts to slow down as well as in the main downstream current. Again, you have the benefits of food, comfort and safety.

5. Dams and Falls

In places where water drops vertically over an obstruction, it digs a deep safe hole for fish. In addition, such places are difficult for fish to climb over, so that fish moving gradually upstream to cooler water or to spawn, tend to bunch up just below dams and falls.

6. Big Rocks and Boulders

These not only break the current—giving fish resting places
—but there are also deep holes just below them and often
undercuts on their sides. Both of these offer fish safety.
Places studded with big rock slabs and boulders are always
prime sections of any stream.

7. Overhanging Bushes or Trees

Since most river fish's enemies attack from above, the fish prefer some overhead cover. Then, too, overhanging foliage or dead-falls give shade as well as protection—a condition most fish seek on bright, sunny days. Even where the water may appear shallow, such places are always worth trying.

8. Undercuts

Another, and often more productive, form of cover is created where currents undercut banks or rock ledges. Such
places, especially cuts under the roots of big, bankside trees,
are the safest of all in the river. The biggest fish like to take
over these lairs and repel all intruders.

13. Pockets

Large rocks or boulders emerging, or almost emerging, from rapids, dig downstream holes creating mini-pools. These can be surprisingly productive, despite their small size—especially during midday or in hot weather.

14. Shady Spots

On summer afternoons when the rest of the river seems dead, you can often get interesting fishing early in the afternoon by fishing north-south sections with high shading hills to the west of them. By using a map or by exploring, you can often find such sections and extend your fishing day.

15. Tails of Pools

Late in the evening, often just before it gets too dark to see, fish will drift down the pool and feed at the lip where it breaks out into the next rapids. This is seldom a good location early in the day, but it can offer the best sport of the day on a late summer evening.

16. Dancing Pyramids

Where slow water meets fast, a series of small, stationary, dancing waves will occur. Food drops to the bottom here, and large lazy fish will take over these patches—if there's enough depth. Even if depth and cover are lacking, fish are still likely to feed in such places at dusk.

17. Standing Waves

When you see one or a series of stationary "bumps" or
waves in a fast run or a rapid, you can be sure there's an
obstruction—probably a submerged boulder—directly upstream. Trout, especially rainbows, like such lies—so give
them extra attention.

FRESH WATER

Little Fish

If you take a small fish from a place that looks like a choice big-fish spot, move on. Something's wrong. The place just isn't as good as it looks. There are probably no big fish there because large specimens do not allow small ones within five or ten feet of their lie.

Check it Out

During midday—especially on warm, sunny days—it pays to walk through water you expect to fish that evening. You will discover fish lies you would never have noticed by looking at the surface. If you wade in swimming trunks you can feel the colder water from springs, too.

FRESH WATER

Rising Water

Many streams and rivers seem to go dead during low water and hot weather. However, if you time your trip to arrive right after a good rain when the water is rising and cooling, you can often enjoy fishing that rivals the best you had in springtime.

PONDS AND LAKES

Still waters are harder to "read" than flowing waters. There are no tell-tale currents to help you discover where the food is concentrated. Then too, lakes and ponds are usually quite deep, making it harder to pick out fish-holding places.

Another problem is that since there are no currents to bring food to the fish, still-water species have to cruise around to find food and moving targets are notoriously harder to hit. Therefore, it's particularly important to learn all you can about the habits and habitat preferences of the type of fish you are after. You will find the vital statistics on the most popular fresh-water fishes on pages 61 through 75.

The majority of still-water fishes, like the smallmouth bass, feed in fairly shallow water early and late in the day, retreating to deeper water as the sun and temperature get higher. Some, like pike and pickerel, spend most of their time hiding in the shallows waiting for their prey to come to them. And a few members of the trout family spend most of the summer in the cool depths feeding on schools of deep-water baitfish.

The successful pond and lake fisherman, no matter where he travels, is the one who knows the territorial and temperature preference of the fish he's after, figures in the time of day or year and, above all, uses his eyes. There are always a surprising number of clues to show him the secrets of the flat and baffling sheet of water in front of him. You will find some of the most important of these on the following pages.

1. Points of Land

A peninsula jutting out into the water offers you two benefits. First, it gives you larger areas of the depth that fish prefer along both of its sides. Second, and equally important, fish cruising the shoreline will tend to pass through a small area off the underwater tip.

2. Islands

Like points of land, islands give you increased areas of fish-
holding and fish-feeding territory. Fish tend to remain near
such places in good quantities. Clues to underwater con-
tours and depths are given by the above-water terrain as described in other parts of this section.

3. Cliffs

Like steep banks, cliffs tell you to expect deep water below them. And one thing more: it is also fairly certain that pieces of rock have crumbled off the cliff over the years building up a productive area of rubble and boulders along the bottom.

4. Edges of Pads

Small fish, which feed on insects that live on stems of lily-pads and weeds, attract hungry big fish. The shade created by dense patches of pads is also an attraction. Fish along the outside edges and in the larger openings so your line will not get fouled so often.

5. *Underwater Weed Beds*

Shallow weed beds can often be seen below the surface; deeper ones have to be located by trolling. Weeds give food and protection to small fish that are sought after by big predators like pike and bass. Work weed beds carefully and thoroughly—especially the edges.

6. *Drift Lines*

On windy days you will often notice distinct lines on the water's surface. These are caused by fast-drifting surface water, and are most often downwind—sometimes extending several hundred yards—from points or islands. The surface food concentrated in these lines attracts fish.

7. Coves

With their long shore lines, extensive shallows, and protection from most winds and waves, coves are top food producing areas. Shallow sections should produce warm-water fish, and the deep water off the points is a good bet for big fish waiting to make nightly raids for food.

8. Sunken Islands

Reefs and underwater bars are really islands that did not quite make it. They offer the same fishing advantages as true islands and should get extra attention. Some are marked by buoys. Others can be found on charts or by searching on sunny windless days.

9. Spring Holes

Where cool water boils up from the bottom, it will attract deep-water fishes during the summer—even if the depth is not great. Such places are usually well-kept local secrets, but you may find some by testing temperatures while swimming or by exploring with a mask.

10. Inlet Streams

Inflowing water brings extra food, but just the flow itself seems to attract some fish. Many species, such as smelt in the spring, and trout and salmon in the fall, spawn in running water; so look for concentrations at stream mouths in the appropriate seasons.

11. Steep Banks

Where the land pitches steeply into the water you can expect good depth very close to shore. Fish that prefer deep water, or those driven deep by summer heat, are likely to be in such places. Various depths along the slope should be tested carefully for different species of fish.

12. Gradual Shores

Where the land slopes gently into the water look for shallows well out into the lake. Such water, especially if the bottom is sandy, is often unproductive. But if there are boulders or weed beds, give them extra attention for they may hold most of the fish in that area.

13. Bait Fish

You will often notice that schools of minnows, small sun-fish or perch tend to hang out in a certain area. Big fish that like to feed on them may not be nearby during the bright hours of the day, but be sure to fish such areas carefully at both dawn and at dusk.

14. Boulders

Big roundish underwater rocks—especially those over a yard in diameter—provide shade and hiding places for fish both large and small. Crawfish like such places, too. Fish every sunken boulder carefully and, if you find a cluster of them, you have hit a hotspot.

Deeper Does It

If you are fishing what appears to be the best places and still are not catching any fish, try farther out from shore. The fish are usually deeper, rather than shallower, than you would expect—especially at midday or during summer when the surface water gets hot.

FRESH WATER

Try Nights

During midsummer, when most vacations take place, fish often bite poorly. If working deeper, cooler water does not produce, try fishing at night. This tactic can be especially effective with largemouth and smallmouth bass. Surface lures are usually best.

Get A Fish's Eye-view

It's a smart idea to explore a clearwater lake or pond with
swimsuit and mask at midday during warm weather. You
will not only locate some unnoticed sunken weedbeds, reefs,
rocks and drop-offs, but you are apt to spot many fish for a
later try.

Fresh-water tackle

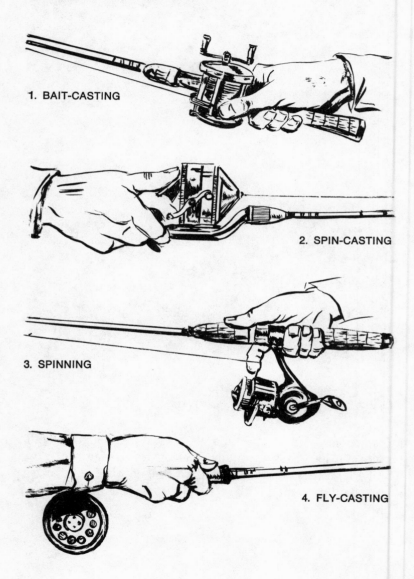

1. BAIT-CASTING

2. SPIN-CASTING

3. SPINNING

4. FLY-CASTING

Fresh-water bait

1. LIVE MINNOW
(hooked through back)

2. LIVE MINNOW
(hooked through lips)

3. DEAD MINNOW
(rigged to spin slowly)

4. WORM OR NIGHTCRAWLER
(hooked lightly)

5. TADPOLE

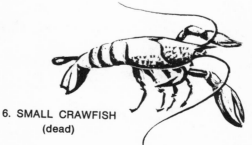

6. SMALL CRAWFISH
(dead)

Fresh-water bait

7. CRAWFISH
(live)

8. HELLGRAMMITE

9. GRASSHOPPER

10. GREEN FROG

11. EARTHWORMS

Fresh-water lures

1. DRY STONEFLY

2. STONEFLY NYMPH

3. CADDIS GRUB

4. HAIRWING ROYAL
   COACHMAN

5. PARMACHENE BELLE

6. RED AND WHITE
   BUCKTAIL

Fresh-water lures

7. MEPPS SPINNER

8. COLORADO SPINNER

9. CANADIAN JIG FLY

10. PLASTIC WORM

11. SPOON

Fresh-water lures

12. WEEDLESS SPOON

13. POPPER

14. FLOATING/DIVING
PLUG

15. SINKING PLUGS

Some Popular Fresh-water Fishes

Before you look through the pictures and vital statistics on some of the more common inland species, you should know how the rating system works.

Size: "Small" does not mean necessarily that the specimen you catch will be bait-sized. Brown trout have been classified as small, for example, because the majority of the fish taken by anglers will weigh under one pound—even though the world record is over 39 pounds. Similarly, you may take a half-pound muskellunge even though the average is over 10 pounds.

The simple rating system we have adopted for this book is that if the average specimen is under one pound, the fish is classified as *small*. If from one pound to seven, it is rated *medium*. If it commonly exceeds seven pounds, we call it *large*.

Range: We have listed the areas where the fish is commonly, but not exclusively, found. Many species have been transplanted to non-native areas. Then, too, some cold-water species are occasionally found far south of their usual range due either to extremely high altitudes or exceptionally low temperatures created in the tail races of deep impoundments.

Depth: This should be interpreted as meaning the usual depth the fish prefers under summer conditions when most fishing is done. Of course, all fish in streams live at quite shallow depths so these are still-water ratings.

Granted, some species like trout and landlocked salmon may be caught in the shallows or at the surface very early or very late in the season. But during most of the fishing season they will be in relatively deep cool water and their rating reflects this habit. And that is why our next heading is so important.

Temperature: We have listed here the temperature F. (Fahrenheit) at which that species feeds most actively. Of course, many fish like perch and pike are caught through the ice when temperatures are in the 30's. Our rating should tell you the temperature (and therefore, depth) fish will seek as surface waters heat up.

Habitat: Some fish have pronounced choices for places to lie or feed. Pike and pickerel love weeds, for example. Others like perch and landlocked salmon tend to wander all over a lake at a certain depth and are much harder for the angler to locate.

Food: Since most fish live on insects and even smaller food when they are fry, this heading needs some qualification also. The items listed are those preferred by adults of catchable size and are given in the order of their importance.

In short, this section is meant to give you the most helpful information in the shortest form. It is not intended as a definitive work on the life-styles and habits of these species.

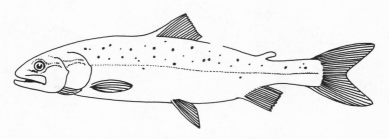

ATLANTIC SALMON (Large)

Range: Eastern Canada
Depth: Shallow
Temperature: Cool, 50's, 60's
Habitat: Runs and pools

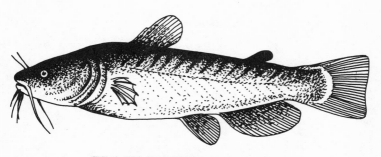

BLACK BULLHEAD (Small)

Range: Eastern half of U.S.
Depth: Shallow, medium
Temperature: Warm, 70's
Habitat: Muddy bottoms
Food: Insects, minnows, mollusks

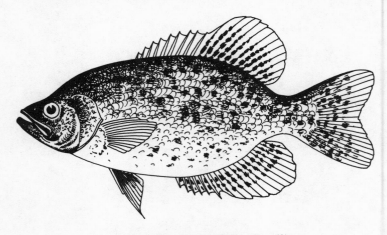

BLACK CRAPPIE (Small)

Range: Eastern half of U.S.
Depth: Shallow, medium
Temperature: Warm, 70's
Habitat: Grass and weeds
Food: Minnows, insects

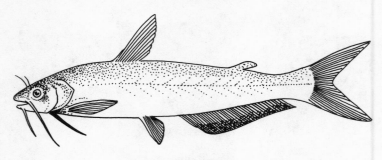

BLUE CATFISH (Large)

Range: Central U.S.
Depth: Shallow
Temperature: Warm, 70's
Habitat: Fast, clear water
Food: Fish, crayfish

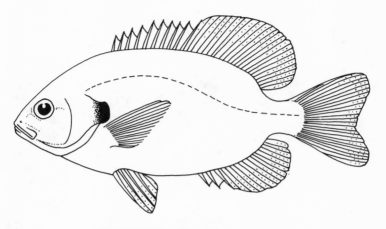

BLUEGILL (Small)

Range: All of U.S., southern Canada
Depth: Shallow to medium
Temperature: Warm, 70's
Habitat: Rocks, weeds, docks
Food: Insects, very small minnows

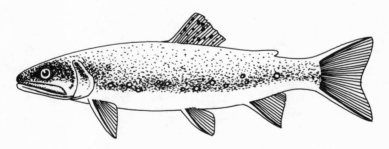

BROOK TROUT (Small)

Range: Eastern U.S., Canada
Depth: Medium, deep in lakes
Temperature: Cool, 50's
Habitat: Wanders
Food: Insects, minnows

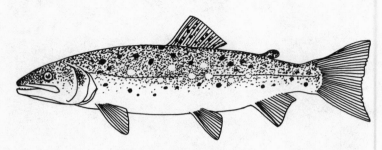

BROWN TROUT (Small)

Range: Northern U.S.
Depth: Medium, deep in lakes
Temperature: Medium, cool, 50's, 60's
Habitat: Near cover in streams
Food: Insects, minnows

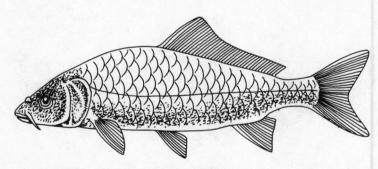

CARP (Medium, Large)

Range: Introduced, entire U.S.
Depth: Shallow
Temperature: Warm, 70's, 80's
Habitat: Mud and weeds
Food: Vegetation, insects

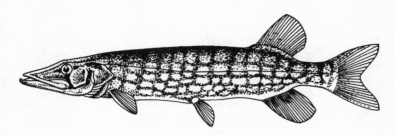

CHAIN PICKEREL (Medium)

Range: Eastern half U.S., S. Canada
Depth: Shallow
Temperature: Medium, 60's
Habitat: Weeds and lilypads
Food: Minnows, small fish

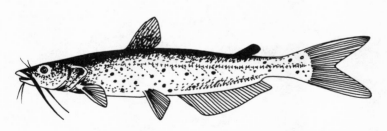

CHANNEL CATFISH: (Medium, Large)

Range: Eastern half of U.S.
Depth: Shallow
Temperature: Warm, 70's
Habitat: Large rivers
Food: Fish, crayfish

CUTTHROAT TROUT (Small, Medium)

Range: Pacific watershed
Depth: Medium
Temperature: Cool, 50's
Habitat: Brooks, rivers, lakes
Food: Insects, minnows·

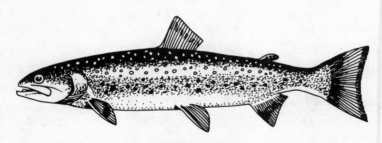

DOLLY VARDEN (Medium, Large)

Range: West Coast drainage
Depth: Deep
Temperature: Cool, medium, 50's, 60's
Habitat: Deep lakes, streams
Food: Minnows, insects

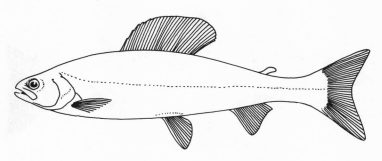

GRAYLING (Small, Medium)

Range: Alaska, Western Canada
Depth: Near surface
Temperature: Cold, 40's, 50's
Food: Insects

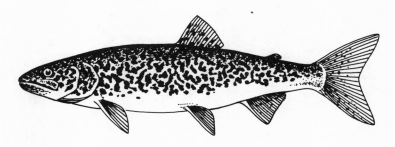

LAKE TROUT (Large)

Range: Northernmost U.S., Canada
Depth: Deep
Temperature: Cold, 40's, 50's
Habitat: Wanders
Food: Minnows, small fish

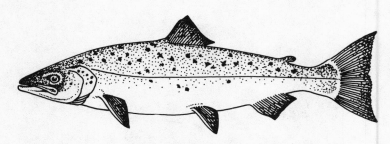

LANDLOCKED SALMON (Medium)

Range: Northeastern U.S., S. Canada
Depth: Deep
Temperature: Cold, 40's, 50's
Habitat: Wanders
Food: Minnows, insects

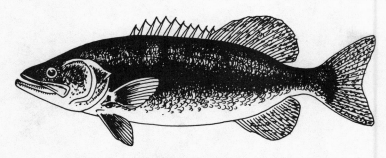

LARGEMOUTH BASS (Medium)

Range: All of U.S., southern Canada
Depth: Shallow to medium
Temperature: Warm, 70's
Habitat: Weedbeds, boulders, snags
Food: Minnows, crawfish, frogs

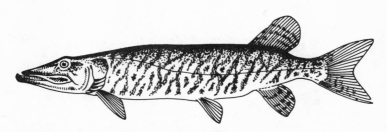

MUSKELLUNGE (Large)

Range: Northern U.S., S. Canada
Depth: Medium
Temperature: Medium, 60's
Habitat: Weeds and snags
Food: Good-sized fish

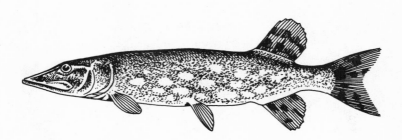

NORTHERN PIKE (Large)

Range: Northern U.S. and Canada
Depth: Shallow to medium
Temperature: Medium, 60's
Habitat: Weed beds, snags
Food: Small to medium fish

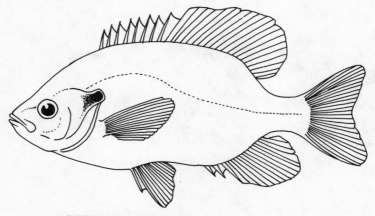

PUMPKINSEED (Small)
Range: Most of U.S., Southern Canada
Depth: Shallow
Temperature: Warm, 70s
Habitat: Weed beds, docks, logs.
Food: Insects, small mollusks, fishes

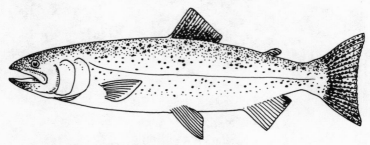

RAINBOW TROUT (Small)

Range: Northern U.S.
Depth: Medium, deep in lakes
Temperature: Medium, cool, 50's, 60's
Habitat: Wanders
Food: Insects, minnows

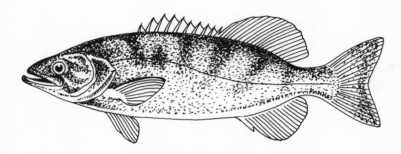

SMALLMOUTH BASS (Medium)

Range: Northern U.S., Southern Canada
Depth: Shallow, medium
Temperature: Medium, 60's
Habitat: Near rocks, rocky bottoms
Food: Crawfish, minnows, insects

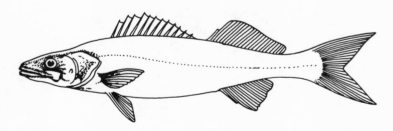

WALLEYED PIKE (Medium)

Range: Northeastern U.S., S. Canada
Depth: Medium to deep
Temperature: Medium, 60's
Habitat: Wanders considerably
Food: Large minnows

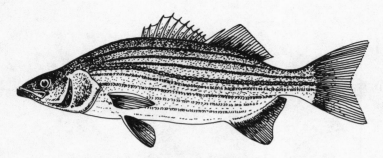

WHITE BASS (Small, Medium)

Range: Central U.S.
Depth: Shallow in evening
Temperature: Warm, 70's
Habitat: Wanders in schools
Food: Minnows, insects

WHITE CRAPPIE (Small, Medium)

Range: Central U.S.
Depth: Medium
Temperature: Warm, 70's
Habitat: Sunken brush
Food: Minnows, insects

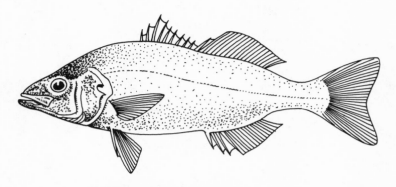

WHITE PERCH (Small)

Range: Northeastern U.S.
Depth: Medium, deep
Temperature: Medium 60's
Habitat: Mud bottom
Food: Insects, crustaceans

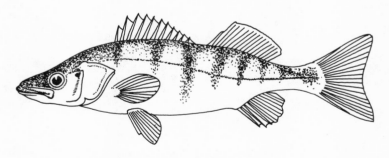

YELLOW PERCH (Small)

Range: Eastern, Central U.S.
Depth: Medium
Temperature: Warm, 60, 75
Habitat: Travels in schools over many areas
Food: Insects, small minnows

SALT WATER

BAYS AND
ESTUARIES

These are the areas where fresh and salt water usually meet. Estuaries certainly are a first mixing point of the two types of water; but many, or even most, bays have a touch of fresh water influence.

How does this affect the fishing—and the fishermen? In several ways.

Let us take estuaries first. The strong influence of fresh water here has a great attraction for some fish. Tarpon, snook, striped bass, to name a few, have a well-known urge to enter brackish, or mixed, waters. These waters are also, in spawning season, concentration points for anadromous species: salt-water fish who spend most of their lives in the ocean, but must spawn in sweet water. Some of these are shad, the herrings, salmon and sea-run trout.

Surprisingly, some purely fresh-water species like the largemouth bass can tolerate quite a bit of salt water. There are estuaries in the South where you can catch largemouth and snook on successive casts.

Bays, with or without pronounced fresh-water influence, have a few extra things in common. Mainly, they are protected from the ravages of storms and pounding waves. This makes them ideal nurseries for many species of fish and crustaceans—all of which are fodder for bigger and better fish. Also, their shallower waters warm up more quickly in the spring or during summer days, raising the metabolism rate—and feeding needs—of many warm-water species.

By all means, read the next section of this book *Surf and Shore*. A few of the tips in that section can also be helpful to bay and estuary fishermen—and every angler these days needs all the help and advice he can get.

1. Narrows

Currents speed up where the water is pinched. This digs a deeper channel for fish protection and concentrates the food moving through into a narrower, easier-to-get-at area. Except at dead-high or dead-low tides when water movement ceases, these are hotspots.

2. Piers and Pilings

With their weed attachments they not only provide food for small fishes and crabs, they also create protective eddies when currents are running. Small fishes plus barnacles, periwinkles, mussels and oysters that often grow on piers and pilings make these structures choice spots.

3. Moving Patches

Schools of fish like mackerel and a few others can be so tightly packed that they actually color the water—even when they are a few feet below the surface. Some bait fish do this also. Always follow and cast such places until you are sure your eyes are playing tricks.

4. Strange Ripples

These can be created by school fish also, but only when they are very close to the surface. Even when the light is bad, you can spot these slight surface disturbances. Ripples can be caused by a school of bait fish or by predators. Get to such suspicious breaks fast and start fishing.

5. *Birds*

Wherever bait fish are pushed to the surface or boil up
wounded from deep water, sea birds will gather quickly.
Fishermen who follow close behind should do well. If the
minnows seem frightened to the surface, fish shallow. If
they're boiling up wounded, fish deep.

6. Brackish Ponds

These may hold significant quantities of catching-size fish only occasionally, but they are important as nurseries and as food supplies. Where they empty into bay, ocean or tidal river, you can expect fish to be positioned for easy pickings —especially at low tide.

7. Channels

Fish often follow channels in and out with the tide, not only because the water is deeper, but because the food-bearing currents are stronger. Anchor just off the edge and fish into deeper water. Buoys often mark channels. It's illegal to tie up to them, but smart to fish near them.

8. Other Boats

One of the surest ways to find good fishing spots is to watch where other boats go. Anglers who fish an area regularly know where the fish are—or where they *usually* are. Nobody can complain if you follow their example. But you can become unpopular if you crowd in too close.

9. Bends

Tidal rivers, like fresh-water rivers, dig deep and tend to undercut their banks on the outside portions of bends. Most food will funnel through such places and their extra depth and overhead cover make them choice holding places for many types of game fish.

10. Backwaters

Where tidal currents flow in a direction that is opposite to the main flow—as they often will for short distances just below sharp points or obstructions—food will tend to drop to the bottom. Schools of bait fish tend to gather here, attracting bigger predators.

11. Jumping Bait Fish

Whenever you see a shower of minnows in the air, get to the area and start fishing quickly. Bait fish don't jump because they need the exercise. They are trying to escape from danger—usually big fish that are lurking below and are actively feeding.

12. Swirls

On calm days or in the evening, you will often see a boil or boils on the surface. This usually means that a fish has taken a shrimp, swimming crab or minnow just below the surface. The bigger the swirl, the bigger the fish. Be guided by that if you have a choice of boils to cover.

13. Bay Entrances

Where bays empty into the ocean—often through a narrow cut or channel—there will be a strong current to pull food in and out, according to the tide. The biggest fish in the bay, including some visitors from the ocean, are likely to hang out here.

SALT WATER

Chum

When fishing is poor or slackens off, even though you are in a choice spot, it often pays to try to attract fish and start them feeding again. Extra bait or crushed clams, mussels, crabs, etc., parceled out down current will usually start the action.

Stir Things Up

Even if you have no chum or spare bait aboard, you can
often attract fish—especially bottom feeding types—by
dragging your anchor in a small area. This works best over
a sand or mud bottom. It uncovers bottom food and the
clouded water itself will usually draw some fish.

SURF AND SHORE

Here, you are on the rim of a vast ocean. There is no influence of fresh water. Nor are the relatively shallow inshore stretches protected from surf or storms.

And this, perhaps, is what makes fishing from beaches and rocky shores so exciting. On all but rare calm days waves created hundreds, even thousands, of miles away hammer away at the shoreline.

It is the power of these waves that creates a special type of fish-feeding. It sets up powerful currents. It churns up the sand temporarily exposing crabs, sand eels, sand bugs, shrimp, etc., giving feeding fish sudden targets of opportunity.

Whether you fish from the shore itself or offshore from a boat, there is one important fact to remember. Many types of small fish migrate up the coastline in spring and down again toward warmer water in the fall. This creates a "river" of fish—some earlier in the season than others—up and down the coastline for most of the year. Newspaper and radio reports will usually tell you what part of this migration, and how concentrated, is in your area.

The ocean can be dangerous to waders and boaters, so be careful, be watchful, and be prepared. You are trespassing on the edge of an area where even large ships have disappeared. But this is also the place where the biggest fish of all live and that adds an extra zest to fishing.

1. Offshore Breakers

Where waves break a good distance offshore and there is a relatively calm patch of water between them and where the waves finally hit the shore, you can be sure there is some relatively deep water between the breakers. Here is a natural place for food, bait fish and game fish to collect.

2. Throats of Tidal Ponds or Creeks

At ebb or low tide, salt creeks and ponds pour strong currents into the ocean—carrying a stream of crabs, shrimp and minnows with them. At times like these, such places are hotspots, but at a high, or flooding, tide they may provide only so-so fishing.

3. Points

These are natural fish-concentrators because schools, or single fish, cruising the coastlines tend to pass by just off the point. And when tides are running slightly crossways to points, you get an extra bonus: they tend to create big eddies that hold bait fish, drift food and game fish.

4. Other Fishermen

Many other fishermen you see are locals with local knowledge and experience. Fish near them (observing a decent
interval) or where you have seen them fish and you will
cash in on old-timers' knowledge. (You will also find most
of them fishing in places described in this section!)

5. *Dancing Waves*

Where two currents—even light ones—collide, a stationary patch or strip of small dancing waves will occur. Food will tend to collect or drop to the bottom in such places, attracting feeding or just lazing bait fish, which in turn will attract the hungry predators you are after.

6. *Dark Patches*

These usually mean weed patches or clumps of rocks with weeds attached. Rocks hold crabs, mussels, barnacles, etc., while weed offers protection for minnows and other types of feed. If there are only a few of these in a sandy area, fish them hard and pay special attention to the edges.

7. Lines of Spume or Flotsam

These visible trails usually mean the edge of a tidal current
—often one so slight that it leaves no other traces. Debris
attracts bait fish and smaller marine organisms. Bigger fish
are attracted in turn. And some fish, like dolphins, lie in the
shade that is created.

8. Jetties and Breakwaters

These structures not only give shore anglers access to deeper water, they also have special fish-attracting qualities of their own. Their rock structure offers hiding places for crabs and fish and they create currents and eddies that bunch bait fish and other food.

9. Cliffs

There are almost always boulders and rock slabs on the
ocean bottom below rock cliffs—whether you can see them
or not. Years of storms and surf have quarried these from
the rock face. Such places are favorite haunts of striped
bass, tautog and many other species.

10. Dark Water

Deep water is a different color from shallow water. It is usually a darker green or deeper blue. Many fish—especially during daylight hours—hang out in deeper water than you would expect, so give the deeps extra attention if the shallows are not producing any action.

11. Roily Water

Some portions of the shoreline are more susceptible to erosion than others and here the surf stirs up bottom silt and food while nearby areas remain clear. Fish the edges, not the centers, of such patches. Fish enjoy the extra food here, but dislike getting sand in their gills.

12. Tidal Rips

Points of land, sunken sandbars, underwater channels, and the like, can funnel tidal flow into easily seen temporary "rivers." Their faster flow and usually greater depth attract fish looking for either food or safety. Fish find such places quickly so fish them carefully.

13. Bait Schools

Wherever you notice a concentration of small fish—whether in an eddy, off a jetty or seen through a wave in the surf—cast quickly. Fish eat fish. If you want to do the same, give extra attention and effort to places where bite-sized specimen gather.

SALT WATER

Incoming Tides

If you have a choice of fishing time, take the flood tide. This does not hold true in all situations, of course, but fish usually feel bolder, feed more heavily and work in closer to shore when the water is getting deeper than they do when it's shallowing.

Try Nights

Most hospitable and accessible shorelines attract so many bathers and boaters during the summer that game fish are often driven off into deeper water. All this changes after dark when the crowds are gone. Big fish often raid the shallows for food after dark.

After a Blow

Major storms can often muddy the inshore water so badly that fishing is ruined. But a good blow or mild storm, in most areas, quickens the surf and stirs up extra food. If the water remains reasonably clear, this is a prime time for the surf caster.

Salt-water reels

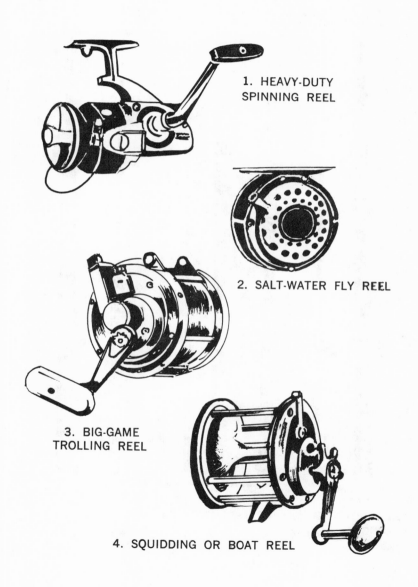

1. HEAVY-DUTY
SPINNING REEL

2. SALT-WATER FLY REEL

3. BIG-GAME
TROLLING REEL

4. SQUIDDING OR BOAT REEL

Salt-water tackle

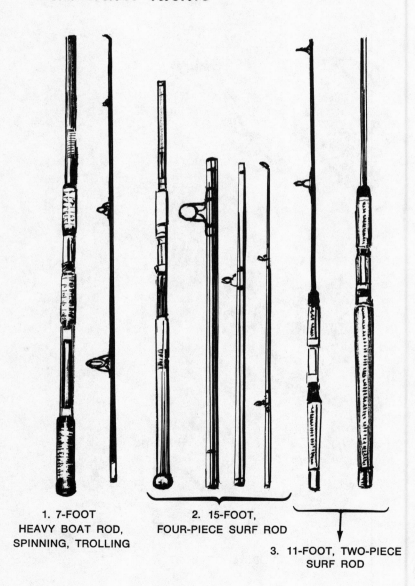

1. 7-FOOT
HEAVY BOAT ROD,
SPINNING, TROLLING

2. 15-FOOT,
FOUR-PIECE SURF ROD

3. 11-FOOT, TWO-PIECE
SURF ROD

Salt-water bait

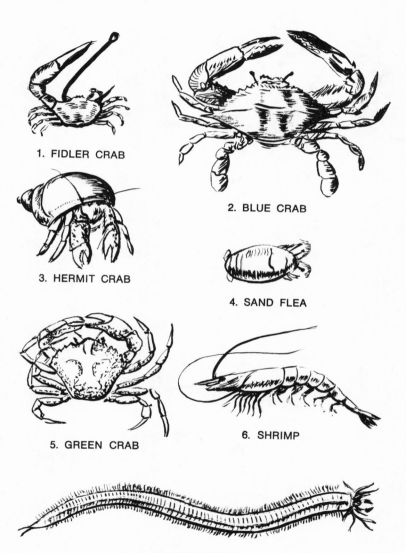

1. FIDLER CRAB

2. BLUE CRAB

3. HERMIT CRAB

4. SAND FLEA

5. GREEN CRAB

6. SHRIMP

7. SAND WORM

Salt-water bait

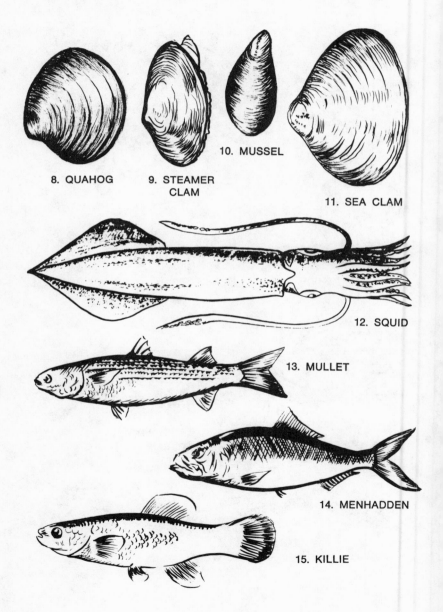

8. QUAHOG

9. STEAMER
   CLAM

10. MUSSEL

11. SEA CLAM

12. SQUID

13. MULLET

14. MENHADDEN

15. KILLIE

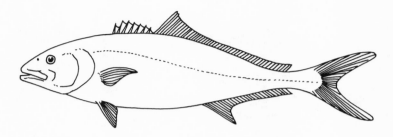

AMBERJACK (Medium, Large)

Range: Southern Atlantic
Depth: Medium
Habitat: Wanders
Food: Small fish

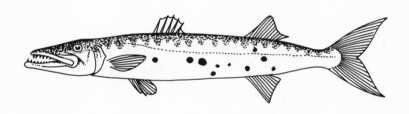

BARRACUDA (Medium, Large)

Range: Tropical, both coasts (several species)
Depth: Near surface
Habitat: Cruises deep water reefs and rocks in shallows
Food: Medium sized fish

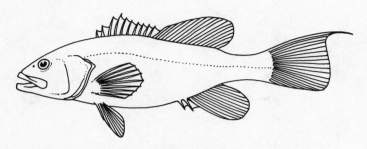

BLACK SEA BASS (Small)

Range: Central Atlantic
Depth: Medium
Habitat: Hard bottoms, wrecks
Food: Mollusks, crabs, minnows

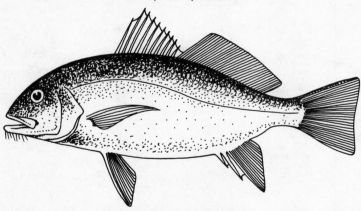

BLACK DRUM (Medium, Large)

Range: Southern Atlantic and Gulf of Mexico
Depth: Shallow
Habitat: Sandy shores, bays
Food: Clams, crabs, shrimps

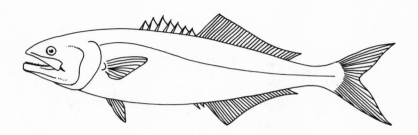

BLUEFISH (Medium)

Range: Entire Atlantic Coast
Depth: Medium to surface
Habitat: Wanders in schools
Food: Small fish

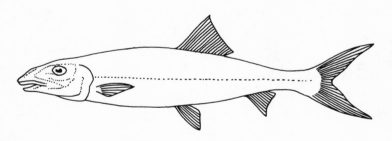

BONEFISH (Small, Medium)

Range: Florida, Bahamas and South
Depth: Very shallow
Habitat: Sandy or grassy flats
Food: Clams, crabs, shrimp, minnows

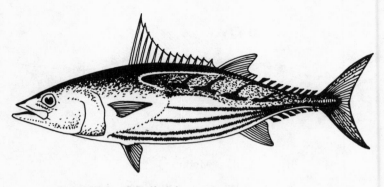

BONITO (Medium)

Range: Pacific, Southern Atlantic
Depth: Near surface, medium
Habitat: Wanders in schools
Food: Small fish

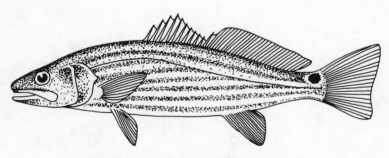

CHANNEL BASS (Medium, Large)

Range: Southern Atlantic and Gulf of Mexico
Depth: Shallow
Habitat: Bottom
Food: Crustaceans, mollusks, fish

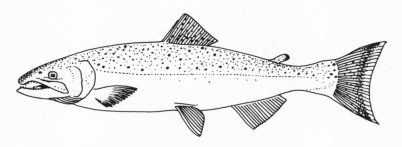

CHINOOK SALMON (Large)

Range: Pacific, California to Alaska
Depth: Medium, deep
Habitat: Bays, estuaries
Food: Small fish

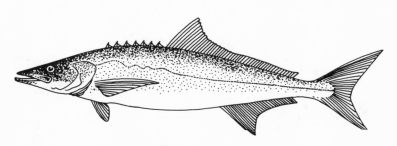

COBIA (Medium, Large)

Range: Southern Atlantic
Depth: Shallow, medium
Habitat: Buoys, pilings, flotsam
Food: Crabs, shrimps, small fish

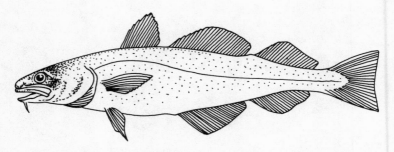

COD (Large)

Range: Northern waters, both coasts
Depth: Bottom, deep water
Habitat: Over banks
Food: Small fish, shellfish

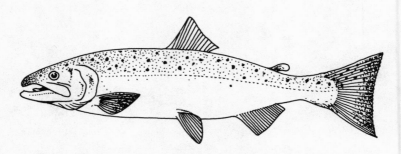

COHO SALMON (Medium, Large)

Range: Pacific Coast, Great Lakes
Depth: Medium
Habitat: Bays, estuaries
Food: Small fish

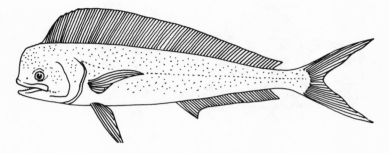

DOLPHIN (Medium, Large)

Range: Southern Atlantic
Depth: Near surface
Habitat: Under floating weeds, flotsam
Food: Small fish

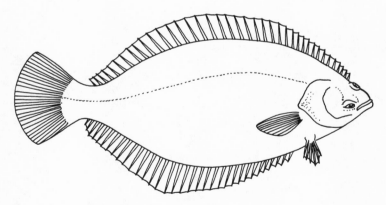

FLOUNDER (Small)

Range: Northern Atlantic Coast
Depth: Shallow
Habitat: Muddy, sandy bottoms
Food: Worms, crabs, shrimps

JEWFISH (Large)

Range: Southern Atlantic
Depth: Shallow
Habitat: Coral heads, caves
Food: Fishes

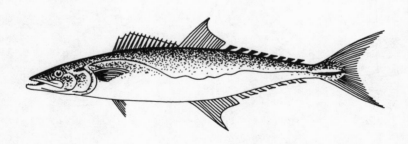

KINGFISH (Medium, Large)

Range: Southern Atlantic
Depth: All depths
Habitat: Wanders in schools
Food: Shrimp, small fish

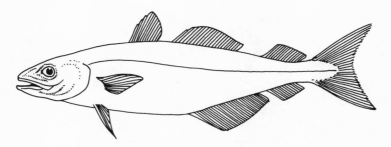

POLLACK (Medium)

Range: Northern Atlantic
Depth: Medium
Habitat: Wanders in schools
Food: Small fish, shrimps

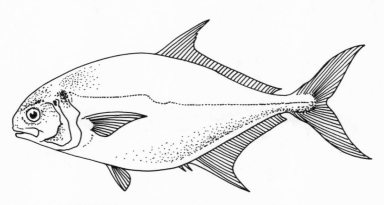

POMPANO (Small)

Range: Southern Atlantic and Gulf of Mexico
Depth: Shallow
Habitat: Sandy beaches, inlets
Food: Shrimps, crabs

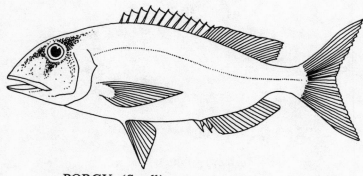

PORGY (Small)

Range: Northern Atlantic Coast
Depth: Medium
Habitat: Bottom
Food: Small crustaceans, worms

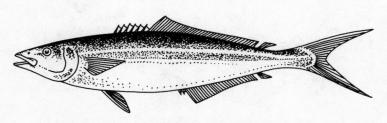

RAINBOW RUNNER (Small, Medium)

Range: Tropical waters
Depth: Shallow, medium
Habitat: Wanders
Food: Small fish, crustaceans

ROOSTERFISH (Medium, Large)

Range: Southern Pacific
Depth: Shallow, medium
Habitat: Sandy beaches
Food: Small fish

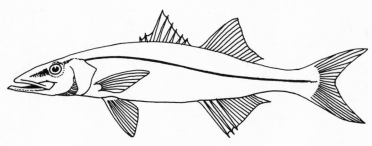

SNOOK (Medium)

Range: Warm Atlantic, Gulf of Mexico, Pacific
Depth: Shallow
Habitat: Brackish bays, rivers
Food: Small fish, crustaceans

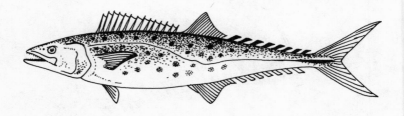

SPANISH MACKEREL (Small, Medium)

Range: Southern Atlantic
Depth: Shallow, medium
Habitat: Wanders
Food: Minnows, shrimp

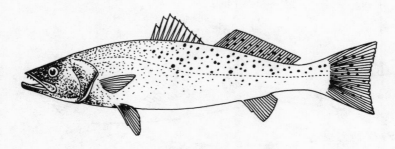

SPOTTED WEAKFISH (Small, Medium)

Range: Southern Atlantic, Gulf of Mexico
Depth: Shallow
Habitat: Weedy bays and tidal rivers
Food: Shrimp, crabs, minnows

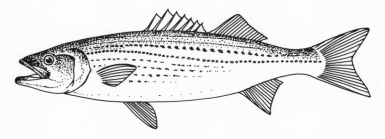

STRIPED BASS (Medium, Large)

Range: Mid-Atlantic, Mid-Pacific Coasts
Depth: Shallow, medium
Habitat: Brackish bays, coastlines
Food: Fish, crustaceans, clams

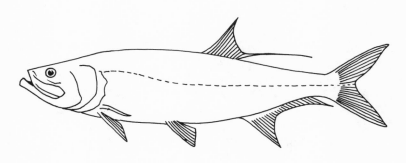

TARPON (Large)

Range: Southern Atlantic Coast
Depth: Shallow
Habitat: Brackish bays, lagoons, rivers
Food: Small fish, crustaceans, shrimp

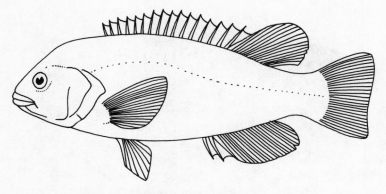

TAUTOG (Small, Medium)

Range: Northern Half Atlantic Coast
Depth: Shallow
Habitat: Rocks, mussel beds
Food: Barnacles, mussels, crabs

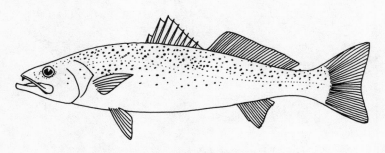

WEAKFISH (Small, Medium)

Range: Mid-Atlantic Coast
Depth: Shallow, surface to bottom
Habitat: Shallow, sandy areas
Food: Worms, shrimps, crabs, minnows

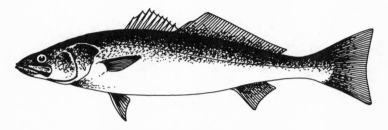

WHITE SEA BASS (Medium, Large)

Range: Central to Southern Pacific
Depth: Medium
Habitat: Near kelp beds
Food: Fishes, crustaceans, squid

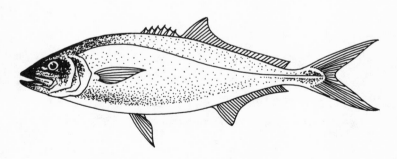

YELLOWTAIL (Medium)

Range: Southern Pacific Coast
Depth: Near surface
Habitat: Wanders in schools
Food: Small fish

Useful Knots

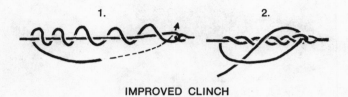

IMPROVED CLINCH

LARKS HEAD

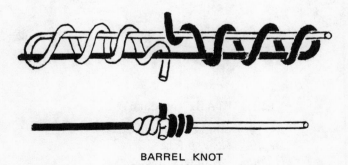

BARREL KNOT

Useful Knots

IMPROVED END LOOP

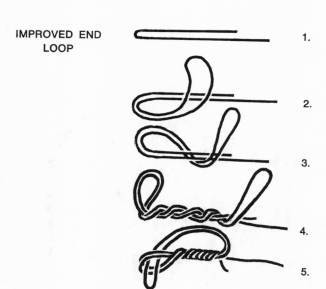

1.

2.

3.

4.

5.

PERFECTION LOOP KNOT

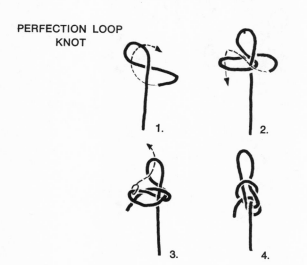

1.

2.

3.

4.

Hooks

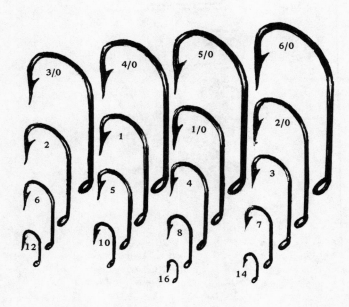

Hooks

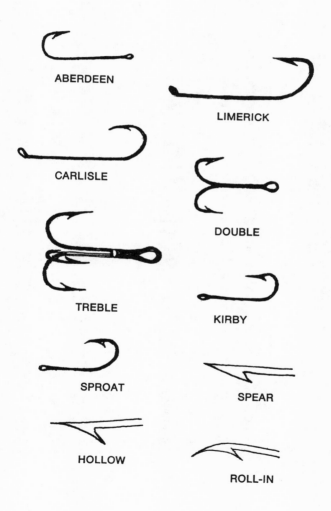

ABERDEEN

LIMERICK

CARLISLE

DOUBLE

TREBLE

KIRBY

SPROAT

SPEAR

HOLLOW

ROLL-IN

The Anatomy of a Fish

1. NOSTRIL

2. GILL COVER

3. GALL BLADDER

4. KIDNEY

5. PYLORIC CAECA

6. INTESTINE

7. BODY CAVITY LINING

8. DORSAL FIN

9. AIR BLADDER

10. MUSCLE TISSUE

11. LATERAL LINE

12. ADIPOSE FIN

13. CAUDAL FIN

14. ANAL FIN

15. VENT

16. URINARY BLADDER

17. PELVIC FIN

18. TESTIS

19. ADIPOSE TISSUE

20. SPLEEN

21. STOMACH

22. LIVER

23. PECTORAL FIN

24. HEART

25. GILL

26. MAXILLA

27. MANDIBLE

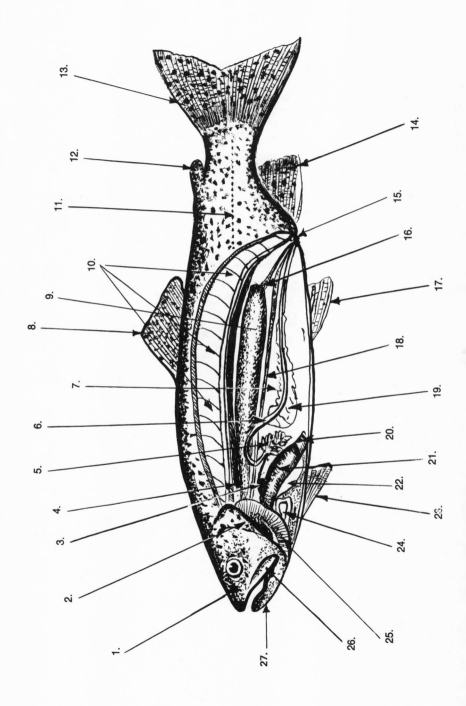

HOW TO CARE FOR AND CLEAN YOUR CATCH

Kill your fish (a sharp blow just behind the eyes with a stick will kill most small species); gut it and remove the gills as soon as possible after you land it, for inner parts spoil quickest. Put it on ice or in a refrigerator as soon as you can. *Do not* leave it in water, even though the water may seem cool.

If you have no ice keep the fish dry and in the shade. Be sure it gets a good circulation of air around it. (Even with these precautions, fish can spoil in a few hours when the temperature is over 70 F.) Fish, unlike cheese and wine, definitely does *not* improve with age. Unless you are going to freeze or smoke it, the sooner you eat it the better it will taste.

Following are some of the simpler, more popular ways of cleaning fish.

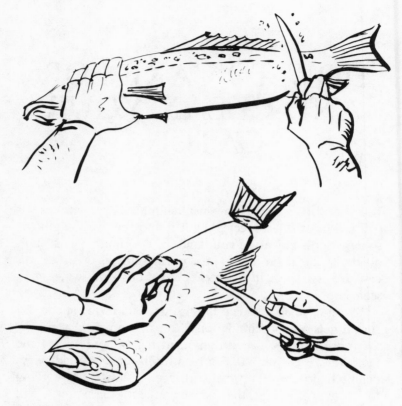

Scaling

This is the easiest way to prepare sunfish, perch and other pan fish for frying. Use a scaler or a sharp knife held perpendicular to the fish and stroke firmly from tail to head. The fresher the fish the easier the scaling. Run the knife fairly deep along each side of both dorsal and anal fin to pull them free. Finally, slice off the head with a diagonal cut from back of the head down toward the vent and remove the remaining viscera.

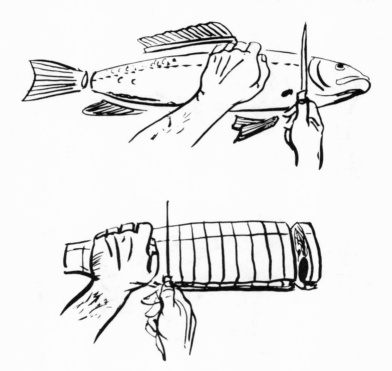

Steaking

Large fish are often steaked for grilling or broiling. Scale fish and remove major fins (see p. 146). Clean out viscera. Place fish on a board and with a sharp knife cut cross sections of desired thickness, starting just behind the head and working down toward the tail.

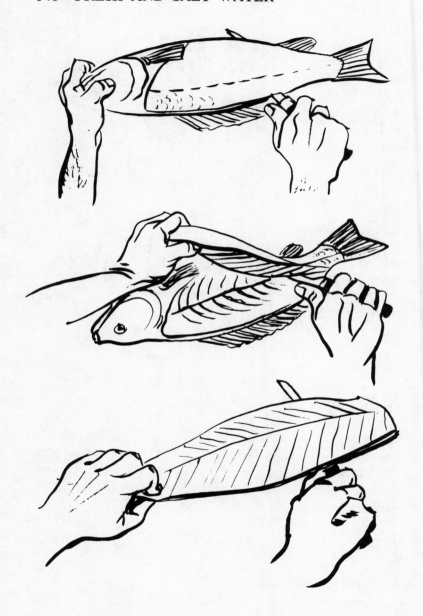

Filleting

Place fish on board and cut on an angle just behind the head down to, but not through, the backbone. Slice along backbone (but not through rib cage) to a point just behind the vent. Now push the knife through to the opposite side and run it with a sawing motion along the backbone until the flap of flesh is cut free at the tail. If the fish is small, cut off fillet where the ribs start; if large, run the knife down over rib cage to cut a full fillet.

Lay fillet skin-side down on a board and, starting at the tail, angle the knife blade toward the skin and work forward until you have freed the fillet from the skin.

Place the fish on the board again and repeat the filleting process on the other side. When you have finished you will have two boneless, skin-free slabs of flesh.

Filleting is easier if you use a well-sharpened special filleting knife.

Now, enjoy your catch.

About the Author

LEONARD M. WRIGHT, JR., is Advertising Promotion Manager of *The New York Times*, and has written extensively on the subject of fishing for leading sports journals. He is the author of *Fishing the Dry Fly as a Living Insect* and *Fly-fishing Heresies*.